D0359144

ders

To my beloved children Tal, Laliv and Tamar

The Soul Bird

Michal Snunit

**Illustrated by
Na' ama Golomb**

ROBINSON
London

Deep down,
inside our bodies,
lives the soul.
No one has ever seen it,
but we all know it's there.
Not only do we know it's there,
we know what's in it, too.

Inside the soul,
right in the very middle of it,
there's a bird standing on one foot.
This is the soul bird.
It feels everything we feel.

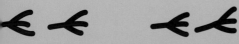

When someone hurts our feelings,

the soul bird runs round and round in pain.

When someone loves us,
it hops and skips
up and down
backwards and forwards.

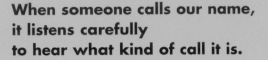

When someone calls our name,
it listens carefully
to hear what kind of call it is.

When someone is angry with us,
it curls itself into a ball
and is silent and sad.

And when someone hugs us, the soul bird,
deep down inside, grows and grows
until it almost fills us.
That's how good it feels when someone
hugs us.

Deep down, inside, lives the soul.
No one has ever seen it,
but we all know it's there.
Never, never has a person been born
who didn't have a soul.
It sparks the moment we are born
and never leaves us—
not even once—
for as long as we live.
It's like the air that people breathe
from the moment they are born
until the time they die.

Do you want to know what the soul bird is made of?
Well, it's really quite simple:
it's made of drawers.
These drawers can't be opened just like that–
because each is locked with its own special key!
Only the soul bird can open its drawers.
How?

Ah, that's quite simple too:
with its other foot.

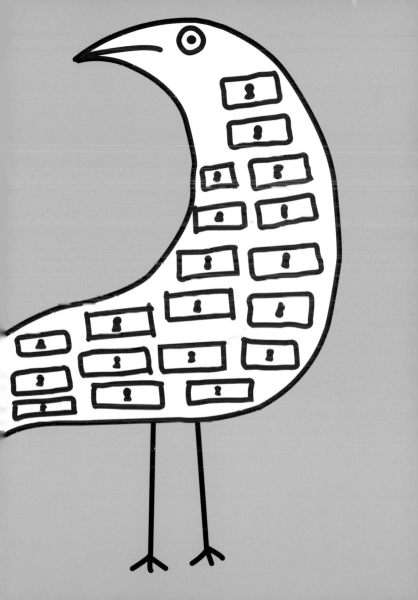

The soul bird stands on one foot,
and with its other foot
(tucked under its wing when
it's resting) it turns the key to the drawer
it wants to open,
pulls the handle, and lets everything
inside – out!

Because there is a drawer for everything we feel,
the soul bird has many, many drawers:
one for being happy and one for being sad;
one for being jealous and one for being content;
one for being hopeful and one for being hopeless;
one for being patient and one for being impatient.
There is also one for hating
and one for being loved.
There is even a drawer for being lazy and one for
being vain.
And there is a special drawer for your deepest
secrets –
which is hardly ever opened.
There are other drawers too –
whatever drawers you dream of.

Sometimes you can tell the bird
which keys to turn
and which drawers to open.
Sometimes the bird will choose especially for you.
Like, when you want to be silent
and order the soul bird to open the silence drawer.

But the bird decides all by itself
to open the talking drawer
and you talk and talk
without even wanting to.

You want to listen patiently, but the soul bird
opens his impatience drawer
and you become impatient.

Sometimes you get jealous without meaning to.
And sometimes you get in the way when you only want to help.
The soul bird does not always do what it is told
and gets things in a mess.

By now you've understood that everyone is different
because there's a different soul bird deep inside.
The bird which opens the happiness drawer each day
pours happiness into your body
and you will be happy.

**But if the bird
opens the anger drawer
he will be angry
until the bird
closes the drawer
behind him.**

A bird who feels bad will open up the drawers which make you feel bad.

A bird who feels good will open up the drawers which make you feel good.

Most important is to listen to the soul bird, because sometimes it calls us and we don't hear it.
This is a shame – it wants to tell us about ourselves.
It wants to tell us about the feelings that are locked up inside its drawers.

Some of us hear it all the time.
Some almost never.
And some of us hear it

only once in a lifetime.

That's why it's a good idea–
maybe late at night when everything is
quiet–
to listen to the soul bird
deep down inside us.

Constable & Robinson Ltd
3 The Lanchesters
162 Fulham Palace Road
London W6 9ER

First published in the UK
by Robinson Publishing
1998

This edition first published
in the UK by Robinson,
an imprint of Constable &
Robinson Ltd 2004

Text copyright © EL-AZ
Ltd and Michal Snunit
1998, 2004
Illustrations copyright ©
Na'ama Golomb 1998, 2004

The moral right of the
author has been asserted.

A copy of the British
Library Cataloguing in
Publication data is avail-
able from the British
Library.

ISBN 1-84119-107-8

Printed and Bound in
Singapore

3 5 7 9 10 8 6 4 2